How To
FEEL GOD'S
LOVE
& be Happy

Rev J Martin

ISBN-10: 1727665287
ISBN-13: 978-1727665284

DEDICATION

I dedicate this book to my Dad who recently passed away. He never knew it but he was the main inspiration for all my books. May he rest in peace.

CONTENTS

ACKNOWLEDGMENTS

This book would not have been possible without the support and encouragement of my family, and the inspiration from my Heavenly Father.

A special thanks to my editor, all the people a Pixal Design Studios for the lovely design work, and Amazon for providing the digital tools by which I can translate my message to the world.

Finally, I would like to thank YOU, for buying my book, may it enlighten your life and bring you peace and happiness.

Introduction

In life, we all want to feel Gods love and be happy but achieving this can be difficult. We can have all the money in the world, we can have our health, we can have endless opportunities, but still, the stresses of life can bring us down.

When I was younger, I used to be very hot-tempered. People always seemed to have a way of winding me up. What annoyed me the most was the fact that I didn't want to feel that way. I wanted to be calm. I wanted to be relaxed. I wanted to have a deeper connection to God, yet I didn't seem to be making much progress.

Most people only love others if there are specific criteria met. Their attitude reflects ideas like, "You can only be my friend as long as you live by my rules." "I will only speak to you if you have the same outlook on life as me."

Instead, we need to make allowances and adapt to see the glory of God. It's only when we live by the teachings of Jesus will we live a life of health, happiness, and peace of mind. The measure we give is the measure we receive. Don't let feelings of negativity get between you and a friend, a co-worker, or a family member. Don't let the enemy get a foothold in your life. Don't let feelings of anger, frustration, or disappointment grow within your spirit and bring about division.

Cast aside old destructive attitudes and embrace the new.

When you learn what is keeping you from God's love, what is keeping you from happiness, what is keeping you from fulfilling your destiny. Watch as a whole new world opens up to you.

What Is Keeping Us From Gods Love?

The main obstacle keeping us from Gods love and the feelings of happiness is our relationships with others. People can frustrate and annoy us to a point that we can take no more. This can lead us to say and do things that we wouldn't normally. We may be in the right but holding on to negative feelings in the end helps no one.

God made us all differently; we all have different views and handle issues in our own distinct ways. Some of us are very well organized, planning our lives weeks in advance. Others, conversely, may leave everything to the last minute.

If two people with these mindsets live under the same roof for example, it is safe to assume that their personalities will clash and there will be tempers flaring from time to time.

Just because someone doesn't approach a situation the same as you doesn't mean that they are wrong and you are right - you just have different views of the world. So be aware that this difference will cause friction, usually at the worst possible time.

An exception to this is if someone is abusive or controlling; you should always confide with a friend or counselor if someone makes you feel scared or threatened.

Depth Of Character

It shows a high level of maturity when you can get along with those that have different views to you, not arguing over the issues that separate you.

Sometimes you have to be the "bigger person" and notice why there is friction in the first place. This way, if it does arise, you can highlight that it's not personal; it's your different natures that caused it.

We can't expect relationships to be perfect. No matter how much you get on with someone, if you are around him or her long enough, there is always a chance of being hurt or offended by them eventually. One minute you can be top of the world. Then someone close to you does something that infuriates you, you see red, and your whole mood changes.

For example, you feel annoyed that they upset your perfect morning and they feel upset because you're not as responsible as they would like. If the blame game starts, a small problem can quickly escalate to the point that you're questioning yourself about how a beautiful morning turned into an argument over something that happened years ago. No one was in the wrong; differences of opinion just came to a head and an argument broke out.

Colossians 3:13 NLT
Make allowance for each other, and forgive anyone who offends you.

Get All You Need

The most important relationship that we need to work on is our relationship with God. Through His word, we can get all the encouragement that we need.

In Exodus 16, the people of Israel were hungry and discouraged. They grumbled to Moses, saying, "If only we had died by the Lord's hand in Egypt! There we sat around pots of meat and ate all the food we wanted, but you have brought us out into this desert to starve this entire assembly to death."

We can all relate to this. Not literally, but in a metaphorical manner. For example, there are times when we feel that God has abandoned us. It can feel as if our world is falling down around us. However, even if we are hungry like the people of Israel were, the word of God is all the food that we need.

Proverbs 4:20-22
My son, pay attention to what I say; turn your ear to my words. Do not let them out of your sight keep them

within your heart for they are life to those who find them and health to one's whole body.

There are many ways to improve our relationship with God. The first is to speak to Him through prayer and ask Him for reassurance and love.

Another powerful way to improve our relationship with God is to read the Bible. The amount of wisdom that it contains is refreshing. Reading the words of the apostles and prophets gives us great insights into the best ways to live.

We should also keep God's commandments, as doing this will bring you closer to Him. Obey them and eternal happiness is yours. Disobey them and you may suffer the consequences.

John 14:21
Whoever has my commands and keeps them is the one who loves me. The one who loves me will be loved by my Father, and I too will love them and show myself to them.

Seeing With Love

It's easy to be critical of people if they don't live up to our expectations. However, when we are critical or judgmental of others it can block Gods love and keep us from happiness.

We can think things like, "that person is so annoying, why do they have to be so loud? Why do they always have to take over conversations?"

We think this way largely because we would never act in such a way. However, when we criticize, we are disapproving of how a person lives their life. Do not judge, and you will not be judged- Luke 6:37. Instead, find ways to lift people's spirits, helping them to believe in their gifts and abilities, saying things such as "I believe in you" and "you're talented and you will achieve great things." It will surprise you how people respond when they know that you care.

The simple act of helping others has helped me to deal with depression and anxiety, as it takes my attention of myself onto others.

Eyes of Jesus

Everywhere Jesus went, He saw potential in people that didn't see it in themselves. He didn't focus on their weaknesses or faults; He saw the glory of God at work. Jesus knew that you never bring out the best in a person by telling them what they are doing wrong or by telling them what they ought to do. Criticizing or condemning others doesn't create lasting change, unless it is given in a loving and constructive manner.

You bring out the best with love. You bring out the best with compassion. You bring out the best by showing people that you care.

Your friends and family may do things that annoy you or that you don't agree with, but you don't have to berate them for it. Instead, focus on what they are doing well and encourage them to do even better.

If you treat people with the understanding, love, and respect that you yourself would like to be treated with, they are more likely to listen to what you have to say and follow your example.

New Perspective

When people get into a relationship, romantic or otherwise, there is a lot of respect in the beginning. Then over the years, that respect can break down, and the love for each other can fade. Criticism can replace compliments, and before long the relationship can deteriorate.

From today, let the people in your life know what you think of them. If they make you laugh, smile, or give you support, let them know. Don't take them for granted. A few words could make their day.

Be free with your compliments. It may seem like a person knows how much you appreciate them, but don't assume anything. Let the people in your life know how much they mean to you— we all crave attention, admiration, and compliments.

Inspired by Others

If you compliment people on excellent service, whether they're a cashier, waitress, or local taxi driver, they will remember you for it. Out of the thousands of people they deal with on a weekly basis, they will sometimes even remember your name.

The main thing that people remember about you is how you make them feel, so leave them with a positive feeling. Build people up where ever you go; being a positive ray of sunshine is much better than being a negative rain cloud. I have found that small gestures like these bring me deep inner happiness.

Have More Peace & Happiness

Romans 15:1
We who are strong in the faith ought to help the weak in order to build them up.

Everywhere Jesus went He encouraged people and He made them feel better about themselves. Praise and encouragement can strengthen the bond between two people. It's incredible what we can achieve when someone believes in us.

Many people's attitude is: "nobody helps me, so why should I help anyone else?" To them, I say, "if you want more peace and happiness in your life, the first step is to help other people have more peace and happiness in their lives. As the saying goes, what goes around comes around." When we help others, God sees that love, care, and compassion, and repays us many times over.

In the Sermon on the Mount, Jesus extended selflessness by loving our enemies and praying for our persecutors. He taught us that it's easy to love a friend or brother—as even unbelievers do that. Love the unlovable, because this is how we become more like God, who gives blessings to everyone.

A few words of encouragement or a listening ear can do more for a person than you will ever know. To you, it's just a moment of your time, but to them, it can be the turning point in their lives.

Extended Selflessness

I'm sure there have been people that helped you along the way. For example, maybe a manager or a friend recommended a course to you, which turned out to be the turning point in your career. They saw potential within you that you failed to see. Although you may not realize it, you can be that person for someone else.

Are you inspiring the people in your life? Are you instilling faith in family and friends? Are you telling them that they can achieve great things?

Maybe some people you know have gotten off course – if so don't give up on them! Make sure they know you are there if they need you. Make sure they know that you believe in them.

You never know when people are at their lowest; a smile can be easily faked and doesn't necessarily reflect what's going on inside them. So, keep inspiring, keep motivating, keep encouraging. One day your faith in them will grow into something special, and one day they will achieve great things. We all need guidance when we have lost our way.

When you show love to others and bring happiness to their lives, you in turn will receive love care and happiness that will help you on your way.

2 Corinthians 9:7 ESV
Each one must give as he has decided in his heart, not reluctantly or under compulsion, for God loves a cheerful giver.

Peace Friendship and Love

Two friends fell out with each other because one of them kept a note of every time the other let him down. On one occasion Brian was very sick, so could not attend a fundraising event organized by Neil. Knowing how he would react, Brian let him know days in advance, thus giving him adequate time to find a replacement.

Because the event didn't go as planned, Neil blamed Brian. He reminded him each day, for months, about how he had let him down. The friendship ended, as Brian could take it no more and he had ultimately done no wrong.

This is what can happen when we remind people of their shortcomings - a relationship can break down if one or both of those involved are subjected to constant criticism, whether supposedly warranted or undeserved.

A person may not be as punctual as you. A person may not be as organized as you. Nonetheless, would you rather have peace in your home and friendships that you treasure?

Real Value

Shannon was driving home one day from work when she turned a corner too sharply and scraped the side of another car. She pulled over, as did the other driver. An elderly gentleman got out, relieved that the accident was not as severe as it could have been.

He went over to Shannon who was still sitting in her car crying. "Are you ok?" He asked. "Yes, It's just that my husband bought this car for me and is going to be very upset.

"It will be ok," the elderly gentleman said, trying to console her. "Your husband will understand." They talked for a few minutes before he asked, "If I could get your insurance information, I'll be on my way."

"I don't even know if I have that,"

"Well, its usually in the glove compartment," the man suggested. "Check there."

Sure enough, that's where it was. Attached to the file containing the insurance information was a note, that read, "Shannon, just in case you have an accident, please remember that I love you. The car can be replaced."

This is the type of person that we should all aim to be like - someone that is considerate, someone that holds relationships in higher regard than material things. Material things, no matter how expensive, can be replaced, yet our loved ones cannot.

It's essential that we show compassion, love, and empathy before anger, disappointment, and frustration. You could be a tidy person and like everything to be in its right place, yet other members of your family may not be this way inclined. Conversely, they leave everything behind them as they go, and you frequently remind them of this irritating fault, saying things like "why do you never put things back in the right place?"

Doing this only upsets you and them, as they will feel that they cannot live up to your high standards. We need to make allowances if we are to have love peace and happiness in our homes.

1 Corinthians 13:4-7
Love is patient, love is kind. It does not envy, it does not boast, it is not proud. It does not dishonor others, it is not self-seeking, it is not easily angered, it keeps no record of wrongs. Love does not delight in evil but rejoices with the truth. It always protects, always trusts, always hopes, always perseveres.

No.1 Happiness Killer

The Bible teaches that we need to adapt and adjust to keep the peace - it doesn't say that other people should adapt and adjust to us. If we want to have peace, we have to be the ones that change.

We can't have the attitude, "if my friend would do what I want them to do, then I would stop reminding them of their faults" or "if only my co-worker treated me right then I would listen to what they have to say."

The key is learning to adapt. We have to be willing to make adjustments and stop waiting for someone else to do it first. We cannot wait for others to make peace on our behalf; we must be the peacemakers.

Revived Marriage

A young couple called Duane and Emily quarreled about a lot of things. They regularly hurt each other's feelings, and Duane found himself sleeping on the couch many nights. They disagreed about their finances, delegating chores, and how they would raise their children. They argued about big things and little things in equal measure.

One day, Emily put all Duane's folded clothing on his dresser so he could put them away. He then asked why she didn't just finish the job and put the clothes away herself. To this, she responded. "I took the laundry to the laundry room, washed your clothes, dried your clothes, folded your clothes, and all you can do is complain. How about a 'thank you' for all the work I've already done?"

It got to the point where they couldn't ask each other questions without the other taking it the wrong way. They rarely complimented each other and often felt unloved.

Despite their challenges, Emily wanted her marriage to last—and so did Duane. Emily loved her husband so much but was tired of being hurt by him, and she was tired of hurting him.

Neither of them knew what to do.

When Emily went to her minister, he recommended that they should go to marriage counseling. When they discussed their matters properly in a controlled environment, it became clear that neither was willing to make adjustments for the other. Nevertheless, when they made some allowances for one another, their relationship was back on track.

Many people get a divorce because they disagree over insignificant things. They allow small problems to escalate and refuse to back down from their point of view.

If you allow disagreements in your relationships to fester over time, then your relationships will slowly get weaker. One day you will wake up and a once-loving relationship will have turned into one where you hardly speak to each other. All of this will happen over a few disagreements that were never resolved.

Maybe you haven't spoken to someone for months, giving him or her the cold shoulder. Life is too short to live that way. If possible, go to that person and make things right— while you still have the chance to. Doing so will allow Gods love to flow into your life.

Regret Is Heavy

I recently spoke to a man that was broken and defeated. When I ask what was wrong, he spoke of a rift he had with his father. They hadn't spoken in over five years.

He knew deep down that it needed to be resolved but he kept putting it off. Then a couple of weeks ago he received a call; his father had died suddenly. You see forgiveness weighs ounces, while regret weighs tonnes.

Don't wait until you cannot make amends with someone. Do it today. Keep the peace. It's not always about being right; it's about doing what is right. You can win every argument, but if it brings about division, if it tears you apart, in the end, you didn't win at all.

I believe God gives us warnings, letting us know deep within that something must change. Reminding us that we need to be patient, be kind, let go of pain, and start acting as a peacekeeper in our lives. "Well, I'll be a peacemaker as soon as my neighbor changes. I'll be good to them as soon as they treat me better."

No. If you wait for someone else to be the peacemaker, you could be waiting a very long time. Most people are stubborn; they would rather hold a grudge than have Gods love and happiness in their hearts.

From Enemy to Friend

Becky and Lindsey worked together but never really got along; Becky was jealous of Lindsey's personality. Although she wasn't as attractive as her, she had a way with people and could get along with anyone.

At every opportunity, Becky would annoy Lindsey about her faith. She would call her a "goody two shoes" and the like. This annoyed Lindsey so much that she would seek revenge, spreading stories about how promiscuous Becky was and stooping down to her level.

One day while praying, Lindsey asked God, "why do I have to work in such a horrible environment? When are you ever going to change Becky?"

God spoke back to Lindsey in the form of a thought. "Lindsey, I will change Becky as soon as you change." "God, what do you mean?" Lindsey cried. "She is the problem, she is the one that starts all the arguments!"

"No. You are not doing all that you can to keep the peace. You know the right thing to do, and when you do it, I will change Becky."

Lindsey took God at his word and started to make an extra effort to keep the peace. Whenever Becky would call her names, make fun of her, or spread gossip, Lindsey no longer argued back or spread stories of her own; she remained quiet and didn't say anything at all.

After a couple of weeks, Becky got tired of making fun of her. It was clear to everyone in the office who was causing all the arguments and giving themselves a bad name.

So often we can be waiting for the other person to change. They might be at fault, but when we add to the situation, we are partly responsible. When we allow friction to exist in our relationships, we close the door on God's love from entering our life.

Forgive and Let Go

A few years ago, I missed an important meeting as a friend gave me the wrong directions for getting there. It was my fault for not double-checking, yet it irritated me. Going about my day, it kept replaying in my mind.

When entering a supermarket, I walked into the automatic doors. The security guard got me an ice pack, and after 10-15 minutes the swelling had gone down. Sitting there, I realized that I had brought it on myself. The management was very apologetic, as the automatic doors didn't open quickly enough, but I knew I was truly to blame for being stuck in my head, per se.

Rather than forgive and forget, I had let a simple mistake consume my thinking. I knew better, yet I continued to hold onto the annoyance and the accident happened as a result of my distracted thinking.

As the scriptures say, don't give a foothold to the enemy, a foothold to unrest, a foothold to un-forgiveness. When we don't let go and forgive, a situation can replay in our minds over and over. This way, negativity can get a foothold, causing a relationship to break down over time.

Un-forgiveness got a foothold so strong on me that day that I didn't look where I was going. Luckily I wasn't driving, as one moment of distraction could have proved fatal to myself or other road users.

When we hold onto negative feelings, we are choosing to step out of God's protection. We step out of God's love and favor. Yes, there are times we must confront issues head-on, but there are times when we must avoid arguments and give up the right to be right. Take the initiative to keep hassle out of your life. Let go of the insignificant things that produce division and discord.

When you swallow your pride to keep the peace, your relationships will flourish. That being said, if you do your best and the other person continues to cause trouble then you must re-evaluate that relationship.

Getting What You Want

We all want good things to happen to us and come into our lives. The best way to do this is to help others. Most people, however, seem to go through life living selfishly, only thinking of themselves.

One of the worst attitudes that we can have is the "me me me" attitude. People who think this way are only interested in serving themselves and furthering their own lives, seeing little point in making others feel happy.

The quickest way to happiness, however, is to take our minds off of ourselves and put our attention onto others. Approaching each day with the attitude of "who can I help, inspire, and bless with my actions today?" Learn to give a little something to others each day.

God created us to help and to serve. Everywhere we go, we should look out for opportunities to be a blessing, it doesn't have to be something big. For example, if the freeway traffic backs up slow down and let that car in which is in front of you. Just be good to people whenever you can. At the grocery store, if the person behind you has fewer items, just let them go ahead of you.

It doesn't necessarily matter if you don't, but you should ideally be on the lookout for ways that you can be good to people. At the forefront of your mind, you shouldn't think "how can I get blessed?" but "how can I be a blessing?" Put simply, be attentive.

Back to School

I've learned that if you make someone else's day better, God will make your day better. If you bring a smile to someone's face, God will bring a smile to your face. This is the most rewarding way to live - not "what can I get?" but "what can I give?"

When you spread love, you are helping to spread Jesus's message around the world. Learn to be good to people, learn to give your time, and learn to radiate wisdom, love, and compassion.

Maybe a friend is going through a difficult time and they said something hurtful to you due to stress. If you have the attitude of "I'm not helping them after what they said to me" then the relationship could irreparably break down.

We need to make allowances for people; we need to be there for them in their time of need. Relationships are not always easy, and sometimes doing what is right is hard, but when you give, you will always receive.

We should have a goal every day to do at least one good thing for someone else. You can't be good to everyone, although you can be good to the people that God puts in your life. Take the time to compliment someone and brighten their day. Kind, loving, and compassionate actions will always speak much louder than words.

Galatians 6:10
Therefore, as we have the opportunity, let us do good to all people, especially to those who belong to the family of believers.

Times Up

One day I was at the airport. An elderly man that couldn't speak any English was going up to people but everyone was just ignoring him. I gestured with my hands to draw what he wanted. He drew a phone with an arrow to a little girl. As a result, I gave him my phone.

Five minutes later a young girl came out of the crowd and ran to hug him. It was clear that she had taken his phone and gotten lost.

A simple act of kindness gave them both so much joy. It might have cost me a little money, but I have learned that when I'm good to other people, God will be good to me. I could have ignored him like everyone else but I have realized that my assignment is to be good to people.

That is one of the main reasons that God has put us here, and if we are going to meet our highest potential we have to make it a priority to be a blessing. Not just in the big things but in the small things too.

Luke 6:38
Give, and it will be given to you. A good measure, pressed down, shaken together and running over, will be poured into your lap. For with the measure you use, it will be measured to you."

Paid in Full

There was a young man that grew up very poor in a small city. He would go door-to-door selling different items to try to pay his way through college. At one point, he only had a dime to his name.

He was very hungry, and had not eaten properly in a couple of days. He got his nerve up, and the next house that he knocked on, he was going to ask them for something to eat.

A very attractive young girl answered the door, when he saw how beautiful she was, he asked for a drink of water instead. She thought he looked tired, so brought him a large glass of milk.

He drank it slowly and asked what he owed her, feeling refreshed and re-energized. But alas she said, "No you don't owe me anything. My mother taught me to never expect pay for an act of kindness."

Leaving the house, he not only felt stronger physically, but his faith in God was strengthened too. He had been on the verge of giving up his education and quitting.

Years later, the young girl became critically ill, but local doctors couldn't find out what was wrong with her. So they sent her to the leading specialist in the city; a man named Howard Kelly. When he heard about the town that she came from, he studied her file more closely. Then he went straight to her room and recognized her at once. From that day, he gave special attention to her case. After a long medical battle, she was eventually cured.

Dr. Kelly requested that the bill was sent to him for approval. He looked at it then wrote a note on the edge of it and sent it to her room. She was afraid to open it, knowing it would take years to pay it off. Finally, she looked and the note caught her attention, it read, "paid in full with one glass of cold milk."

This is a lovely story about how one act of kindness can be remembered, and is based on true events. It shows that if you become a miracle for someone else that is the seed that God will use for your own miracle.

In difficult times, it can be easy to fall into self-pity, worry, and doubt. Instead, get your mind off of yourself and go out and be a blessing for someone else. Even small gestures like giving someone a glass of cold milk or taking the time to listen is all that is necessary.

Ripple of Love

There was a lady that told me a story about something that happened to her when she worked as an attendant at a McDonald's drive-thru. One day a customer pulled up and ordered her morning coffee, when she went to pay, she said, "I want to pay not just for my coffee but the coffee for the person behind me too."

The next customer pulled up and the attendant said your coffee is free today; the lady in front bought it for you.   The man was pleasantly surprised, so he said; "I want to buy the coffee for the person behind me." This continued for the remaining line of cars.

When you are good to people it rubs off on them and your act of kindness can ripple out into the world. When you compliment someone it puts them in a good mood, and they compliment someone else too. This goes on and on like dominos toppling one another over.

There is enough negativity in the world without adding to it; don't have the attitude of "well they were nasty to me so I'm going to be nasty to them."

Develop the habit of being good to people, I assure you that you will be happier, your life will be more rewarding, plus what you give will come back to you.

In your time of need, the right people will be there, the right doors will open, and you will see God's love in amazing ways.

Creating More Time

Philippians 2:4

Not looking to your own interests but each of you to the interests of the others.

It's so easy for us to get caught up in our own lives, and only focus on ourselves. A family member could be in trouble and we can dismiss them as we are so focused on getting something else done. We might say "I've got plans, don't get me off schedule."

Yes, work is important but if you are under so much pressure that you cant give someone 5-10 minutes of your time then you are either bad at time management or have the bad habit of leaving everything to the last minute.

Many people want to improve their relationships, improve their health, and improve their faith but they have the attitude of "how can I get what I want?"

Whenever I feel discouraged, it helps me greatly to reach out to family and friends to see how I can help them. Often their problems are worst than my own. Plus, listening to them can give me ideas to solve my own issues. You're never closer to the Lord's love and protection than when you give to others, helping them on their way.

Stopped By A Brick

Recently I read a story about a successful business executive that was traveling down a suburban street in his new Jaguar. Suddenly, a brick was thrown and it hit his car.

He slammed the brakes and jumped out, grabbing the young boy who had thrown the brick and pushed him to the ground. "Why did you do that?" he screamed. "That damage is going to cost your family a lot of money!

"Please, please…. I'm sorry! I didn't know what else to do!" cried the boy. "I threw the brick because no one would stop!"

Tears were rolling down his face as he pointed to the pavement. "It's my brother," he said. "He fell out of his wheelchair into the road, and I can't lift him up." Sobbing, the boy asked the executive, "Would you please help me get him back into his wheelchair? He's too heavy for me."

The mood was instantly changed when the man saw what had happened. He went over and lifted the young man up into his wheelchair. Then he watched as the little boy pushed him down the sidewalk towards their home.

The young executive never did get the damage fixed, as he wanted to keep the dent as a reminder— a reminder never to be so engrossed in himself that someone had to throw a brick at him to get his attention.

Investing For The Future

If you withdraw more money from the bank than you put in, you will be overdrawn, which usually results in a fine. Similarly, if you don't invest love, time, and compassion into your relationships, there's also a fine - your relationships could fall apart.

Everywhere you go, make it your business to make deposits in people's lives. Encourage them, build them up, and help them feel better about themselves. This is not always easy, as difficult people draw energy out of you. They are not bad people; they just always seem to have a problem that they need you to solve.

Difficult people don't invest in others; they take from them - mainly their energy and time.You will get the feeling that you don't want to be around them for too long. Demanding people don't seem to realize it, but they are actually pushing you away.

No one likes hearing about your problems all the time, as they too have issues of their own. If you are always talking about what is wrong with your life or how bad people are treating you, that's a selfish way to live.

Imagine each of your relationships as an emotional bank account. No matter who you meet, be it a family member, a co-worker, or a friend. Every time you interact with them you are either withdrawing from or depositing into their account. When you compliment someone you are making a massive deposit. Therefore, tell your friend how amazing they look. Tell your husband or wife, " I appreciate all that you do for me." Tell your children how much happiness they bring to your life. You will be amazed at the power of a few compliments.

Sadly, a lot of people do the opposite. They make withdrawals; they criticize and run others down, then are surprised when their life doesn't work out as planned.

Broken Friendship

Once a young man came to me very distressed. His friend asked him to put money on a horse for a bet, but he put it on the wrong one, meaning his friend lost a lot of money.

The young man offered to pay for the lost winnings but his friend said no, and simply kept reminding him of the mistake. What started out as a joke soon turned to bullying, as all their friends and co-workers joined in, damaging his reputation. Within a few months, the friendship had deteriorated beyond repair.

It was not really in this young man's nature to cut someone out of his life, so he needed advice. First, I asked whether his friend apologized for the way that he treated him. He told me that his friend didn't even think that he did anything wrong.

Then I advised him, If someone treats you in a way that makes you feel uncomfortable and you tell him or her so, and they don't take you seriously, then it means that they don't truly respect you. This means that they will mistreat you again.

If you want to build lifelong, loyal friendships, you must learn to make allowances for people. When you continually remind them of a mistake, you may think it will prevent them from making it again, but all it really does is damage that relationship.

Don't embarrass others and do your best to protect a reputation. Everywhere we go, we should make it our business to help people feel better about themselves.

Childhood Memory

When I was young, I remember when the bread man would arrive at my grandmother's house. She would greet him with a big smile and thank him for the lovely fresh bread. You could see that it brightened up his day, and often he would give her a free pack of buns as a gift for us children. When you are friendly to people and help them through the day, you will be rewarded.

My grandmother had a habit of investing in people in this way, and she was always treated with the greatest respect wherever she went. People need your time and energy. You have the power to put a smile on someone's face and a spring in their step, lifting them out of anxiety, worry, or depression.

Proverbs 11:25
A generous person will prosper; whoever refreshes others will be refreshed.

The simple investments that my grandmother made didn't take more than 30 seconds, yet them 30 seconds produced a powerful impact. This is one of the main lessons I learned from her - always make time for people, as the time you invest will come back, with interest!

It doesn't matter how confident someone seems, everyone needs a few words of praise or encouragement. Every time someone encourages us, it pushes us on to change, to improve, to do more. It grows our confidence in our abilities.

A good manager praises people for the things they do right, as he or she knows that when an employee is appreciated, their morale will be boosted and they will continue to work well as they are being appreciated and noticed regarding their efforts. Learn to give compliments freely. Learn to spread love and happiness where ever you go.

Overdrawn

There was a father that always gave his three sons a hard time. His method of parenting was one of guilt, judgment, and criticism. This worked very well until his three boys turned 18. After this point, they would never spend any time with him.

In his later years, he became very ill and was unable to walk due to COPD. Two of his sons didn't even visit him. The third did visit out of guilt and underlying respect for his father.

He had made no deposits in his son's lives, only withdrawals in the form of judgment and criticism. There were no funds of love, compassion, and empathy when he needed it.

Are you overdrawn in any of your relationships? It is never too late to make some deposits! Using guilt, judgment or criticism never works. All it does is push people away from you. When we correct people, we should never belittle them or make them feel insignificant. Whether it is at home, at work, or in social situations. Learn to treat people the way you would like to be treated: with respect, compassion, and love.

Making Better Choices

You can go to church and pray every day, but if you are not showing love to the people in your life, then you are missing the point. Jesus said in Matthew 16 that "if you are going to follow me, take up your cross and follow me. Forget yourself, lose sight of yourself, and forget about your own interests."

You may say, "Well if I don't take care of myself, who will?" Your Heavenly Father will! He can do more for you in a second than you could do for yourself in a lifetime.

Now, I'm not saying that you must forget about your needs and fall out of balance. That's not what I'm talking about. We all have the love of God within us; it is one of the fruits of the spirit. Deep within we are full of, Love. Joy. Peace. Patience. Kindness. Goodness. Faithfulness. Gentleness, and Self-control.

Roman 5:5

And hope does not put us to shame, because God's love has been poured out into our hearts through the Holy Spirit, who has been given to us.

Many people will say, "I don't have any self-control". If you are not going to control yourself, at least be honest with yourself. No one has a total lack of self-control; some just have more than others.

You see, you may have weak self-control right now because you haven't used it, but every time you use it, it gets stronger. You might be weaker in showing love because you haven't focused on it or used it that much. Nonetheless, you have them seeds of greatness within you. God has equipped us for victory.

You want to be a powerful person? Walk in love. You want to get your prayers answered? Walk in love. Do you want health, love, and happiness? Walk in love.

When we make decisions, they not only affect us but they affect the generation around us and the generations that come after us. If you don't make good choices then you are going to end up living with regret.

Vital Lesson

Bert Andrews was a very angry man. He fought with everyone and didn't treat his family with the love and respect they deserved. When he split from his wife, he fought tooth and nail to get what he could. The saving plans for his children had to be cashed in so he could get half of their money.

He acted like a madman, threatening to kill people, as he had to leave the family home due to a legal ruling. Traumatized, his children wanted nothing to do with him.

Bert inevitably held the childrens' mother responsible, despite his own actions being at fault. Whenever he did get a chance to speak to his sons, he would say they were heartless, bitter, and resentful. His sons longed for a father figure but were always disappointed. People like Bert never see themselves in the wrong; to them, the whole world is conspiring against them.

When Bert came to the end of his life, he had very little to look at except regret. No one visited him because he never treated people right. It's really sad when you live your whole life and no one will miss you when you're gone.

And that was because he made choices all throughout his life that did not build relationships. He was mean to people, he was hard to get along with, he was bitter, critical, judgmental, he was abusive, and he paid the price for it.

The thing is, each one of those things was a choice; he lived according to his feelings and many of his feelings were motivated and controlled by negativity.

When I spoke to him I knew that he had a lot of regrets; the way he looked at the pictures of his family clearly demonstrated that he regretted all the criticism, judgment, and pain that he sent their way.

I don't think I will ever forget the sadness of listening to his life story. You see, we rarely realize what we have until it's gone.

When his sons found out about their father being ill, they went to visit him. Even after all the pain he had caused, they found it in their hearts to forgive him.

I share this story because none of us want to be like Bert. Although always being right and getting your way might feel good in the moment, it could cost you everything you hold dear in the long run.

Today I encourage you to grow up. Seek spiritual maturity. Treat the people close to you with love, compassion, and empathy.

The Gospels state that every correct decision you make helps to reverse the results of any wrong decisions you made in the past. So it's never too late to start to make better decisions.

Renewed in Spirit

Too many people have problems in their lives because they want everyone to align with their way of thinking. However, they never say to God, "change me." The result is that they're upset all the time - full of anger and bitterness because they're not happy.

We need to be the kind of person to put on a new self, the kind of person to make better choices, the kind of person to put others before ourselves.

Ephesians 4:22-24
You were taught, with regard to your former way of life, to put off your old self, which is being corrupted by its deceitful desires; to be made new in the attitude of your minds; and to put on the new self, created to be like God in true righteousness and holiness.

When Bert divorced his wife, the question he should have asked was, "how are my actions going to affect my children?" not "how can I get as much as I can to start a new life?" When we are impatient and selfish, very often it will lead to quarrels and fights, which in turn will lead to anger, bitterness, and pain.

John 4:1-3
What causes fights and quarrels among you? Don't they come from your desires that battle within you? You desire but do not have, so you kill. You covet but you cannot get what you want, so you quarrel and fight. You do not have because you do not ask God. When you ask, you do not receive; because you ask with wrong motives, that you may spend what you get on your pleasures.

Unique Destiny
It is upsetting when others don't live up to our expectations or when others seem to be doing better than us. Nonetheless, it's important to remember that God has a unique plan for everyone.

I remember years ago that I wanted to write. In my mind I knew what I wanted; I had a big vision and I thought I had all the knowledge necessary, so I wanted it all to happen straight away. However, I was very insecure back then, and I didn't have the patience or temperament necessary for writing well. Furthermore, I was still trying to work out who I was as a person and a writer.

At that time, I needed something big on the outside to make me feel good about myself on the inside, but God wasn't going to give it to me until I was spiritually mature and ready.

We need to develop the fruits of the spirit so we are strong only then can we be taken to the next level of our destiny.

Feeling God's Love

We can be critical and judgmental with the best of intentions, but when we drop the need to always get our point across, no matter what the outcome. We will be happier, have less stress, and be closer to God. Forgiving people easily can remove the tension that can corrode family bonds, breakdown relationships, and affect our health.

Often when going through a situation I will ask myself what would Jesus do? Jesus would turn the other cheek. Jesus would forgive. Jesus would look past any negativity.

Now I'm not saying let people walk over you but make allowances— don't let relationships end over trivial matters. Step into the new self, learn to accommodate others, investing love, time, and patience into their lives.

Study the people that God has put in your life. Learn to give them what they need not what you need and you will live a life with less stress and more love and happiness.

I believe that if you will make some of these simple changes you will see major improvements in your relationships, in your career, in your mental and physical health. Your faith will increase as there will be more peace, more joy, and more harmony in your homes, and you will live the life of victory that God has in store.

Put love into everything you do and you will receive more love and happiness than you can contain.

I wish you all the best on your journey.

About The Author

I live on the northwest coast of Ireland. I use this medium to share my true voice. I wish to enlighten others and help them to see that God wants the very best for them. We often make it hard for him to enter our lives as we focus on the dark clouds rather than the silver lining.

In this growing digital frontier I just want to shed a little light out into the world to light up peoples lives in the hope that they to will help inspire others which will slowly but surely change the world, even in a small way.

My Other Books

God's Perfect Timing
The Power Of Letting Go
The Power Of Choice
The Power Of Words
The Power of Faith Can Move Mountains
. Let Angels be your Guide

Printed in Great Britain
by Amazon

47730613R00036